BY APPOINTMENT

Balmoral Castle in the 1880s: chromolithograph by T Nelson & Sons

Balmoral Castle today. View from the West with *porte cochère*.

BY APPOINTMENT

THE STORY IN PICTURES OF ROYAL DEESIDE & BALMORAL

PAUL HARRIS

The Press & Journal and Evening Express
in association with
Archive Publications Ltd

First published 1988 by
The Press & Journal and Evening Express
Lang Stracht
Aberdeen

in association with

Archive Publications Ltd
Carrington Business Park
Urmston
Manchester
Production by Richardson Press

Other books by Paul Harris
published by Archive Publications

Glasgow at War
Aberdeen at War
Tyneside at War (with Clive Hardy)
Edinburgh Since 1900
Aberdeen Since 1900

ISBN 0 948946 38 5 (paper)
ISBN 0 948946 39 3 (hardback)

Queen Victoria. Woodcut by Sir William Nicholson, c. 1898

CONTENTS

ACKNOWLEDGEMENTS

This is the third book I have worked on with Aberdeen Journals Ltd and I should again like to thank everyone at the *Press & Journal* and the *Evening Express* who have made so pleasurable the job of putting together this illustrated book. I am particularly grateful to Harry Roulston, Editor of the *Press & Journal*, Tommy Forsyth in the Library, Bob Bruce and Sandy Smith. The newspapers' invaluable store of glass plates, many of them unprinted for half a century, formed the basis for the black and white illustrations in this book. Other contributors are gratefully acknowledged in the list of Sources of Pictures at the end of the book.

Thank you to the staff at the Reference Department, Aberdeen District Libraries, Charles Burnett and Bob Smith.

I would like to record my gratitude to Her Majesty the Queen who has graciously granted her permission to reproduce a number of paintings held in her private collection. Thank you also to the staff at the Royal Library at Windsor Castle and The Royal Collection, St. James's Palace.

Paul Harris
May 1988

An aerial view of the wild, rugged landscape around Balmoral. Crathie Church is in the middle foreground.

INTRODUCTION

Balmoral is certainly not a palace. Neither is it some sort of glorified Highland hunting lodge. And it is decidedly not merely a Royal bolt hole away from the pressures of state south of the border. Although it has, of course, at one time or another served all of these purposes. Today, it is, primarily, a very private place: it is the nearest thing to home for the British Royal family.

Ever since Queen Victoria wrote in her diary in September 1848 her first impression of Deeside — "all seemed to breathe freedom and peace, and to make one forget the world and its sad turmoils" — the British Royal family has enjoyed an unremitting love affair with its Scottish home of Balmoral and the rugged and beautiful surrounding area, now known as Royal Deeside. In many ways this association is unlikely and, even, bizarre. This Highland retreat is a considerable distance from London, far from other Royal homes and remote from any seat of power or influence. The building itself, as a Royal residence, is actually remarkably small and far less pretentious than the country residences of many minor aristocrats and it lacks many modern comforts and amenities. Charles Greville noted on the first visit to Balmoral, the Royal family lived "not merely like private gentle-folks but like very small gentle-folks, small house, small rooms, small establishment". Queen Victoria's eldest son (later Edward VII) made his own feelings as a young man quite clear when he referred to Balmoral as "the Highland barn of a thousand draughts"!

Nevertheless, the annual sojourn at Balmoral is firmly fixed on the Royal calendar and, indeed, marks the end and the beginning of the Royal year. The Balmoral Estate, referred to by Queen Victoria as "the bonniest plaid in Scotland", has often been at the centre of great events and far reaching decisions but it has always been, and most probably always will be, essentially a family home and a refuge from the pressures of work and duty. How all this came about is a tale of some chance and coincidence.

On a cruise to the west coast of Scotland in 1847 (1), Queen Victoria and Prince Albert were attended by the Royal physician, Sir James Clark. The Royal party stopped on Loch Laggan to stay at Ardverikie, Lord Abercorn's shooting lodge. The holiday was not a conspicuous success: it rained incessantly and Royal disillusion was on the point of setting in. Clark, however, had recently despatched his son, who was unwell, to live with Lord Aberdeen's brother and sister, Sir Robert and Lady Alicia Gordon, at their recently built castle at Balmoral on Deeside (4). The Royal party was intrigued when Clark received a series of letters describing the long, sunny days, the bracing climate and the excellent sport. From this point on, the Queen became fascinated by the area, sight unseen, and Aberdeen artist James Giles was commissioned to paint a series of watercolours of the area which served to enthuse all the more.

On October 8 of that year it so happened that Sir Robert Gordon died — choking on a fishbone according to local belief — whilst eating his breakfast at Balmoral and Lord Aberdeen proposed to the Queen that she might consider taking up the lease on the property. Giles was duly commanded to execute more pictures ("I never made any money working to royalty") and he delivered them together with a personal report in London. Sir James Clark was enthusiastic in the matter on health grounds and it was resolved that the lease be taken up — again, sight unseen.

In May 1848 agreement was reached with the Trustees of the Earl of Fife, who owned the property, for a 27 year lease of the Castle. In terms of the lease many of the servants were taken into Royal service, including John Grant, head keeper, William Paterson, gardener, one John Brown, a stable lad, and even Sir Robert's dog, Monk. The Castle's furniture and furnishings were left and even the pictures were left hanging on the walls by reason of the fact that their removal would have demanded immediate and complete redecoration.

On September 5 1848 the Royal yacht *Victoria and Albert* sailed for Scotland arriving at Aberdeen, well ahead of schedule. In Aberdeen, apparently, "all were thunderstruck with astonishment, many challenging the accuracy of the intelligence" when the Royal yacht rounded Girdleness a full twelve hours before her earliest anticipated arrival. Messengers were despatched to summon the dignitaries supposed to welcome the Queen and there was general relief when her Majesty indicated she would not land until the following day. The next morning she stepped ashore (3) to an enthusiastic and noisy welcome and a great progress ensued through triumphal arches of heather, flowers and evergreens. There was breakfast at Cults, lunch at Aboyne and cannons were fired to announce the Royal arrival at Ballater. The final triumphal arch at Crathie proclaimed, "Welcome to your Highland home, Victoria and Albert". The Royal party arrived at 2.45 in the afternoon at Balmoral Castle and were instantly captivated: "It is a pretty little Castle in the old Scottish style", observed the Queen.

In fact, it was the second castle on the site, having been rebuilt by Sir Robert only nine years earlier in a popular French-influenced style which incorporated witch-capped turrets, fancy gables and battlements (4). The Royal couple were clearly delighted — some of their entourage less so. One Lady-in-Waiting was consigned to a cottage detached from the main building and perforce her breakfast was sent over in a wheelbarrow every morning. Many members of the party found the house small and the accommodation cramped. Accordingly, before the stay drew to a close, Aberdeen architect John Smith, who had previously been architect to Sir Robert Gordon, was summoned. Additions and enlargements were to be designed to bring the Castle more into line with Royal requirements.

These requirements notwithstanding, the stay was an enormous success. Albert shot a stag — a Royal no less — and the gardens delighted the Queen. The whole surrounding area was exhaustively explored on foot and by pony and even the heights of nearby Lochnagar were scaled by the energetic Royals. It was a happy and exhilirated party which left Balmoral for Montrose, then the nearest railway station.

Such had been the success of the holiday that Victoria and Albert resolved to seek to obtain the neighbouring estates of Birkhall, Abergeldie and the Forest of Ballochbuie: a purchase price was agreed for Birkhall and a long lease was secured on Abergeldie. Ballochbuie proved more elusive and was not to be acquired until 1875.

The visit of 1849 was no less successful. The sport was good for Prince Albert and the isolation proved a tonic for the Queen. Not everybody approved of this Royal penchant for life in the wilds. Charles Greville noted in his diary: "There are no soldiers and the whole guard of the Sovereign and of the whole Royal family is a single policeman who walks about the grounds to keep off impertinent intruders or improper characters". And, in London, many were finding the preoccupations of the Queen a mite tedious. Lady Lyttelton wrote that the Queen viewed "Scotch air, Scotch people, Scotch hills, Scotch rivers and Scotch woods all far preferable to those of any other nation in or out of this world". She added, somewhat drily, "The chief support to my spirits is that I shall never see, hear or witness these various charms".

By 1852 events were moving fast. The Castle, together with some 17,000 acres, was formally acquired from the Fife trustees for 30,000 guineas and in the September of that year the whole estate was in use: the Royal couple were in residence at the Castle, Sir James and Lady Clark at Birkhall and the Duchess of Kent and her son-in-law Charles of Leiningen at Abergeldie Castle. There was constantly at least one Cabinet Minister in attendance, although their views on that particular necessity they kept to themselves at the time. Lord Malmesbury opined later that Balmoral was "totally unfit for Royal personages" and Lord Clarendon derisorily referred to the activities as "the scramble of rural Royalty". If the Royals were privy to these views, which would seem unlikely, they were totally unaffected by them. The sport was excellent and there were drives, rides and balls. The Queen sketched and painted and Royals, guests and staff erected a cairn on Craig Gowan, the first of many to be placed on surrounding hilltops.

In that August something rather curious and totally unexpected happened. A miserly bachelor by the name of John Camden Nield, who had made his fortune in industry and who was quite unknown to the Queen, died and left a legacy of £500.000 to her. There was some consternation at first but when it was established that the man had no relatives whatsoever Victoria and Albert decided to accept the gift and to use it on the Balmoral Estate.

The first priority was to build a new and more commodious house to accommodate at least one hundred persons just a short distance from the old. On September 8 Prince Albert sent for the architect William Smith of Aberdeen, son of the previously summoned John Smith, who had died in July. Although Smith's assistance was sought it was made plain that the projected great Scottish *schloss* was to be Albert's creation: the Prince provided the basic plans which were worked upon by Smith and his draughtsmen. There were to be two rectangular blocks, joined together corner to corner by a square tower five floors in height. The building was to be constructed from Glengelder granite, quarried on the estate, by local labour overseen by surveyor James Beattie. Smith was to contract the labour and tradesman and the artist James Giles was to check that the whole accorded with the Prince's artistic concept.

The remarkable thing is that this highly unconventional arrangement actually worked — despite many problems. The quarrying work was difficult and the workers even more difficult: they frequently went on strike for higher wages. But by the September of 1853 the ground floor was up and the Queen was able to perform a stone-laying dedication ceremony. Pending completion of the new building the old Castle was retained and so the Royals were able to both enjoy their now customary holiday and to monitor progress (5).
The correspondent of *The Scotsman* reported in October 1853 on progress at the proposed new home:
"PROGRESS OF THE QUEEN'S RESIDENCE. — The Queen's residence at Balmoral is making considerable progress, and promises, without great pretentions, to be a piece of solid and real construction. A correspondent comments on the circumstance, that the Highlanders seem to have a contempt for scaffolding, ropes, or windlass. He says that every block of granite — from two to three feet long — is transported singly on a Highlanders shoulders. Up a narrow platform of boards and tressels to the place where it is to be set, and with considerable celerity, larger blocks are conveyed by four Highlanders, on a couple of poles. Primitive, certainly."

By September 1855 the new house was ready for occupation. The 68 public rooms were all furnished, prepared and curtained — much as they are today. The provision of 14 water closets and 4 bathrooms was lavish by the standards of the time! And there was tartan everywhere. Tablecloths, curtains, wall paper, rugs, carpets and upholstery all bore the marks of the Royal conversion to all things Scottish (6). Even the linoleum in the servants' quarters was tartan. The whole was decorated with thistle motifs, sporting trophies and paintings and etchings of stags, mountains and tumbling water. Victoria and Albert loved it. Again, others were less impressed. Lord Clarendon noted, "the curtains, the furniture, the

This 1844 cartoon, entitled 'Royal Scotch Patronage', illustrates the Queen and Prince Albert's early interest in Scotland and all things Scottish.

carpets . . . are all of different plaids, and the thistles in such abundance that they would rejoice the heart of a donkey".
An important visitor that month was Prince Frederick of Prussia whose aide-de-camp, Count Helmuth von Moltke, wrote home in some surprise:

"Here the Court of one of the most powerful states resides, and that from these mountains the fate of the world is often essentially modified . . . Only one minister is constantly in attendance, at present the Duke of Argyll, quite young and a thorough Scotchman, with red hair. There are no porters, no host of lackeys, not even a sentinel to be seen. I drove straight up to Her Majesty's door, and as I entered the hall, which is ornamented with stags' antlers, I was received by the tones of a bagpipe. Dancing was going on in another hall to these national strains . . . The greatest absence of restraint prevailed. I am going about in a brown travelling coat and black tie; we even continue in that garb at luncheon at two o'clock, and it is only in the evening for dinner that court dress is worn . . .
The great still is very characteristic. No bustle from servants or guests, no carriages."

Notwithstanding von Moltke's criticisms there was general joy within the Royal party at Balmoral later in the month when twenty-four year old Fritz asked for the hand of the fourteen-year old Princess Royal, Vicky. Albert had previously determined that it would be desirable to bring the two families together and the outcome of the visit was held to be hugely successful. A historic engagement picture was duly taken (12), the first of many group photographs of guests and hosts on the lawns at Balmoral.

Although the main house was completed there was much still to be done in the way of provision of outhouses, larders, stables, lodges and so on. Trees had to be planted, gardens planned and glasshouses erected. Albert was absorbed by all these preparations and work continued apace. In 1856 the old Castle was demolished and the ballroom and office blocks were completed. The absorption of Scottish culture consumed the Royal couple. Highland dress was now worn by the Royal family everywhere in Scotland and the Royal children frequently donned it in England. Albert devised his own special tartan — the Balmoral tartan — of lilac, red and black on a grey background.

For Queen Victoria, this was an idyllic phase. The Royals were at one with the environment, their beautiful new home and with each other. The seal was put on their happiness in 1860 when the Prince of Wales arrived at Balmoral to say that he was much pleased with his arranged bride, Princess Alexandra of Denmark.

The visit of 1861 was marked by some extended and adventurous expeditions into the surrounding mountains and glens (Plate IV). The Queen's Journal makes obvious her delight and exhiliration at her Highland adventures:

"A very few minutes brought us to the celebrated ford of the Tarff (Poll Tarff it is called), which is very deep — and after heavy rain almost impassable. The Duke offered to lead the pony on one side, and talked of Sandy for the other side, but I asked for Brown (whom I have far the most confidence in) to lead the pony, the Duke taking hold of it (as he did frequently) on the other side. Sandy MacAra, the guide, and the two pipers went first, playing all the time. To all appearance the ford of the Tarff was not deeper than the other fords, but once in it the men were above their knees — and suddenly in the middle, where the current, from the fine, high, full falls, is very strong, it was nearly up to the men's waists. Here Sandy returned, and I said to the Duke (which he afterwards joked with Sandy about) that I thought he (Sandy) had better take the Duke's place; he did so, and we came very well through, all the others following, the men chiefly wading — Albert (close behind me) and the others riding through — and some of our people coming over double on the ponies. General Grey had little Peter Robertson up behind him . . .

We had travelled sixty-nine miles to-day, and sixty yesterday. This was the pleasantest and most enjoyable expedition I *ever* made; and the recollection of it will always be most agreable to me, and increase my wish to make more! Was so glad dear Louis (who is a charming companion) was with us. Have enjoyed nothing as much, or indeed felt so much cheered by anything since my great sorrow. Did not feel tired. We ladies did not dress, and dined *en famille*; looking at maps of the Highlands after dinner."

The holiday at Balmoral had also been much cheered by the presence of Prince Louis of Hesse-Darmstadt who was visiting. But the great sorrow alluded to in the Journal extract above was not far away. The Royal couple returned to the south and it was not long before Prince Albert began to display the symptoms of typhoid, contracted from the drains at Windsor Castle. On December 14 he died and the effect of his death upon the Queen is, of course, well known. She was never to fully recover from his untimely demise and was to increasingly seek the solace of Balmoral as a place of peace and seclusion away from the travails of the outside world. It also was, of course, dear Albert's own creation and, far from the associations proving painful, the increasingly lengthy Royal stays at Balmoral were to bring Queen Victoria the only peace of mind she could find anywhere.
At Balmoral itself monuments to the memory of Albert began to appear.

In 1862 the erection of a cairn on Craig Lowrigan was commenced and the Royal party climbed to the summit to add stones to the 40 foot wide foundations which had been laid. By the next visit in 1863 the cairn had been finished: a pyramid of white granite 35 foot high inscribed, "To the Beloved Memory of Albert, the Great and Good — Prince Consort — raised by his broken-hearted widow, Victoria R."
The cairn was joined by other monuments including a sculpture in bronze by William Theed (15) and an obelisk. Above the porte cochère appeared a funeral hatchment (16).

Around this time the Queen's Scots servants became more and more important to her. There was Annie Macdonald, daughter of the Balmoral blacksmith, who was her wardrobe maid and later to become First Wardrobe Woman. And there was John Brown.

John Brown's somewhat giddy rise to Royal favourite began on the night of October 7 1863. The Royal party was returning from Loch Muick when the Royal coachman, disorientated through drink, contrived to overturn the Royal carriage. Brown was travelling on the box beside him and events might have turned out somewhat differently had he not been present. In the event, it was Brown who saved the day, sending for help, making a shelter, administering first aid and even producing claret to soothe the frayed nerves of the Queen and her party. Although he had been noticed previously, this was the real watershed in his career.

Surreptitious rumours of some sort of extraordinary relationship between the Queen and John Brown started to circulate in the mid-1860s. Much of this originated in the press on the continent, which did not feel itself restrained in the same way as the English and Scots press. In September 1866 the *Gazette de Lausanne* reported that Queen Victoria and John Brown were secretly married, were cohabiting and that she was carrying his child, the first such rumour to appear in print. This was followed by some irreverent comment in the Scots press, which greatly distressed the Queen, and by lampoons and cartoons in the English press. Like all such press campaigns it had to run its course and, eventually, it simply ran out of steam but, nevertheless, the rumours and stories persist to this day. Certainly, Queen Victoria, unwittingly and somewhat naively, did little to convince her critics that all was being conducted in the manner it should be.

In 1868 a prestigious two volume work was published under the Queen's supervision. *Highlanders of Scotland, Portraits illustrative of the principal Clans and followings, and the Retainers of the Royal Household at Balmoral* was an illustrated work, a sort of Victorian coffee table book which was assured of wide interest then, as it would be today, with its Royal connection. What came as a surprise, however, was not only that the second plate in the book was of John Brown, but that he was pictured against the background of Osborne House, on the Isle of Wight — the only English background in the whole book (110). It was generally felt that there was more to the matter than met the eye.

This publication was followed ,later, in 1884 by the second volume of the Royal memoirs, *More Leaves from the Journal of a Life in the Highlands.* Not only was the book actually dedicated to John Brown in fairly fulsome terms (111), but he featured prominently in the volume in what were regarded, in the hothouse atmosphere of Victorian Britain, as incriminatingly personal observations. These indiscretions horrified supporters of the Queen — and heartily amused others. But this was nothing to the horror which was evinced when it was made known that the Queen was working on a biography of Brown. Everybody in her circle was appalled and made concerted efforts to persuade Her Majesty of the foolishness of the venture. She would not listen to the objections and it took the intervention of the Dean of Windsor, Randall Davidson, to quash the proposal once and for all.

The truth of the relationship will never be known. One thing is certain and that is that Brown had both direct access to and the very real friendship of the Queen. This he enjoyed, in the vacuum left by the death of Albert, to a greater degree than any other male or female among her subjects. In return she was extraordinarily indulgent towards him and his frailties — including his drinking. Once, when he fell flat on his face in front of the Queen as a result of an excess she announced she also had felt an earth tremor! Others were not so tolerant of her personal assistant: on the Royal visit to Dunrobin Castle in 1873 the Duke of Sutherland made the hapless Brown sleep in a dungeon. Much of the antipathy most probably arose from the fact that Brown was totally protective of the person he saw as his personal charge; he was direct to her in a way which was unacceptable in those days, and he completely lacked psychophancy in an age when a monarch found it almost impossible to discern true friends. Unwittingly, Brown distilled the very mixture of qualities certain to appeal to a solitary, isolated widow.

It seems quite likely that the Queen was infatuated by the bluff, gruff and physical Scotsman. He was extensively photographed on the instruction of the Queen and framed pictures of her Highland servant cluttered her desk. Busts and casts of his features were made in large numbers and littered Balmoral, Osborne and Windsor. Immediately following his Mother's death, Edward VII had the photographs, busts and statues destroyed, wherever he could lay his hands upon them. Jealousy or guilt? More likely, simple hatred arising from the fact that Brown had an ill-concealed contempt for the Prince of Wales' dissolute ways and, to add insult to injury, had frequently thrashed his ill-disciplined sons.

It would seem to be unlikely that any sort of physical relationship ever developed between Royal mistress and servant, although many authorities have believed this to be the case. North-east of Scotland historian Fenton Wyness always maintained there had been issue from the relationship and claimed he could even identify descendants of the progeny. It was always his intention to reveal evidence relating to this in a book entitled *Royal Mistress* but this was unpublished at the time of his sudden death in 1973 and the manuscript was never seen again. It is quite possible — if not highly likely — that Brown had issue born "the wrong side of the blanket" but, by the Queen, seems equally unlikely. The simple fact remains, however, that the logistics of the Queen engaging in a physical relationship with her servant — let alone bearing children by him — would have been virtually impossible.

Other writers have advanced a theory which, at first consideration, appears equally unlikely. Tisdall in *Queen Victoria's John Brown* advances the notion that Brown was a medium and this lay at the core of his influence. He maintains that it is a fact that the well known Victorian medium R J Lees was in attendance to the Queen, brought her into touch with her beloved Albert on the other side and suggested to her that Brown could also effect this. Peter Underwood, a well known writer on the supernatural, also believes this and has elaborated the argument in print. Needless to say, any concrete evidence is virtually impossible to find although there is the irreconcilable act of the Queen having burned Brown's diaries after his death: which is certainly strangely at variance with her other actions to preserve his memory.

After Brown's death at Windsor (112) he was buried on his home territory in the little churchyard at Crathie. The Queen placed there a simple headstone of local granite, a thistle carved on the pediment. The main part of the inscription is simple and affectionate. But is there more suggested by the final part?

THIS STONE IS ERECTED
IN AFFECTIONATE
AND GRATEFUL MEMORY OF

JOHN BROWN

PERSONAL ATTENDANT
AND BELOVED FRIEND
OF QUEEN VICTORIA
IN WHOSE SERVICE HE HAD BEEN
FOR 34 YEARS

Born Craithenaird December 8th 1826,
Died Windsor Castle 27th March 1883
"That friend on whose fidelity you count,
that friend given you by circumstances over which you have no control,
was God's own gift."

Is this an allusion to Brown as the spritirual link with another world?

John Brown died in March 1883. Such was the longevity of the Queen that she found many of her most faithful servants expiring around her: replacements were required and two new faces were to be seen at the Ghillies' Ball at Balmoral in 1887. In the swirl of tartan the dusky faces of the Queen's Indian servants — retained to teach her Hindustani — could hardly be missed. If anything, they were more disliked by those around her than even Brown had been and the rise of Abdul Karim was even giddier than that of Brown. Engaged in June 1887, by 1890 he was known as Munshi Hafiz, Abdul Karim, C. I. E., C. V. O. (referred to in the French press as "Le Munchy") and by 1892 was known as Indian Secretary with his own office of clerks (116). Mrs Bernard Mallet, one of the Queen's Women of the Bedchamber, referred to him as "an unctuous Oriental", and even the Queen's Secretary Sir Henry Ponsonby confessed, "These Injuns are too much for me!" For those who had looked forward to the replacement of Brown it was truly a case of out of the frying pan and into the fire!

The year 1887 brought Queen Victoria's Diamond Jubilee which was enthusiastically celebrated at Balmoral. King Leopold of the Belgians travelled to Balmoral to take lunch; on June 22 there was a six course dinner at the Castle; on July 9 a supper and ball and on July 23 a supper, ball and firework display by C F Shirras, firework dealer and pyrotechnist of Aberdeen. And a bronze statue of the Queen facing one of her beloved Albert was unveiled. The celebrations were ably organised by Princess Beatrice's husband, Prince Henry of Battenberg, who had taken upon his shoulders the domestic arrangements at the Queen's various residences. Although she had initially opposed the marriage she came to appreciate Prince Henry's abilities. On October 2 1887 Princess Beatrice gave birth, at Balmoral, to a daughter — the first Royal child to be born in Scotland since 1600. The child was christened in the drawing room at Balmoral and the event was a great source of joy to the Queen. Indeed, the next ten years were to see some lifting of the deep gloom which had enveloped the Royal household. Much of the credit for this must go to the efforts of Henry and Beatrice who devoted their time and energies to the Queen. Entertainers were summoned to Balmoral: *The Mikado* was performed in the ballroom by the D'Oyly Carte Opera Company in 1891 and over the following years there was Beerbohm Tree in *The Red Lamp*, Carl Rosa presenting *Fra Diavolo* and George Alexander in *Liberty Hall*. Balmoral became a regular stopping-off place for a succession of travelling circuses: Pinder's, 'Lord' George Sanger's (59,60), Wombwell's, Bostock's Menagerie and Mr Ginnett's Circus were all patronised by Royalty on Deeside. There were also early film shows which were a source of wonder to the Royal household. Aberdonian pioneers of film, Paul Robello and William Walker, gave performances at Balmoral by Royal command.

One day the Dundee poet and eccentric William Mc Gonagall presented himself at the gates proposing to recite the works of Shakespeare and his own *bon mots* for the benefit of the Queen. He did not gain admittance — which is possibly a shame as this wild and erratic Scotsman might just have appealed.

There was another disaster for the Queen in January 1896 when the death occurred of Prince Henry of Battenberg on a military expedition off the West coast of Africa. Her spirits were temporarily revived later that year by the visit of Tsar Nicholas II and his young wife — formerly Princess Alicky of Hesse and a granddaughter of Queen Victoria. Balmoral was full and a log cabin village was constructed in the grounds to accommodate the Tsar's retinue (118). A historic cinematographic film was made and, despite the wind and the rain and the absence of sport, the Queen enjoyed playing hostess in her Highland home.

But this was the last great occasion at Balmoral during Victoria's reign. Towards the end of the century the weather at Balmoral became conspicuously poor and, following the death of Prince Henry, there was a sad deterioration in the organisation of the establishment and in general standards. The Queen was old and her sight was failing. Liberties were taken. Mrs Mallet observed. "The footmen smell of whisky and are never prompt to answer the bell".

There is evidence that the Queen was also depressed by the Imperial troubles afflicting her Empire towards the end of the century with fighting in the Sudan, on the North West Frontier and in South Africa. For the first time ever, the annual Ghillies' Ball at Balmoral was cancelled. "The war", Lord James of Hereford commented, "engaged her mind almost entirely". In declining health, Queen Victoria spent her 81st birthday at Balmoral in May of 1900. She was now rarely to be seen out and about and in January of the following year she died at Osborne.

The activities of Queen Victoria, and the Prince Consort during the earlier part of her reign, which had formed the focus of visits to Balmoral really set the pattern for succeeding monarchs. Much of the stay in the Highland home is marked by private activities: walking, climbing, picnics, shooting and fishing. The more formal and public aspects of the Royal visits fit into a well established pattern. The inspection of the Guard upon arrival (at Ballater Station until its closure in 1966); attendance at Crathie Church on Sundays and occasional visits to the Crathie fête and sale of work; and, most public of all, the Royal patronage of the Braemar Gathering.

The tradition of the Royal Guard at Balmoral dates back to 1867, the year in which Theed's statue of the Prince Consort was unveiled by the Queen (15). Word came from the Home Secretary in London that Fenians were planning to size the Queen. General Grey rushed troops to the area and surrounded the policies. More police were drafted in and road and rail links were sealed. No murderous Irishmen actually appeared but the exercise did underline the fact that the Queen was seriously exposed and under-protected in her Highland retreat. As a result, construction was started on a barracks at nearby Ballater and a Queen's Guard was instituted for when she was in residence. This tradition has been carried on to the present day although now, more than 100 years later, the Royal Guard is more of a traditional showpiece with electronic surveillance and specially trained police units bearing the brunt of the responsibility. Despite this, the fact remains that the vast Balmoral Estate is a difficult and vast terrain to police and much of the security for the Royal family derives from the protectiveness and shrewdness of the local community who are all eyes and ears in the matter of the privacy and safety of their guests.

Queen Victoria and Prince Albert attended Crathie Church on their very first Sunday at Balmoral in 1848. It is now a well established tradition that members of the Royal family worship at the parish church when in residence (74-6). The foundation stone of the present Church was laid by Queen Victoria in September 1893 (73) and the Royal family were instrumental in raising the money to build this stylish little church on the banks of the Dee. The Queen arranged for the holding of the Crathie Bazaar whereby the magnificent sum of £1200 was raised (72). Relatives in Royal families throughout Europe were enjoined to contribute and stalls at the two day event were looked after by, amongst others, Royal Princesses. The Royals made crafts and handiworks for sale and Prince Henry took photographs at 5s. a portrait. As a result of this fine effort almost half the necessary money was raised and, on June 18 1895, the handsome white granite church building, designed by A Marshall Mackenzie architect of world famous granite-built Marischal College in Aberdeen, was opened for worship.

When their local church requires help, the Royal family are traditionally the first to rally to the cause and in 1955 the Queen Mother organised a fête in the grounds of Abergeldie Castle (106) to raise funds for a new vestry. Every year the Church holds a Sale of Work to raise funds and Royal visitors are, from time to time, to be seen making their way around the stalls (77-8).

The origins of the Braemar Gathering are safely lost in the mists of time but it is said that it dates from the reign of Malcolm Canmore who summoned the Clans in the 11th century to the Braes of Mar for trials of strength, so that he could pick out his "hardiest soldiers and his fleetest messengers". By the middle of the 19th century these informal trials of strength had developed into more formal contests, conducted every year, in the open air, at one of a number of venues on Deeside.

The Braemar Royal Highland Society had its origins in the early part of the century in the form of a procession and programme of social evenings promoted by local joiners. In 1832 the first athletic competitions were held under the auspices of the Society. When Queen Victoria first came to Balmoral in 1848 the games were held in the grounds of Invercauld House and the actual date was delayed to facilitate the attendance of Her Majesty.

The Royal seal of approval came in 1859 when the Queen invited the Society to hold the games at Balmoral at her expense and the Royal venue was added to the other locations at Invercauld, Mar Lodge, Braemar Castle and the Cluny Park in Braemar. In 1866 the title "Royal" was added to the Society's name and continuing patronage was assured.

In the year of her Golden Jubilee, 1887, the Queen again invited the games to Balmoral and there was lavish entertainment. They were also held there in 1898 and 1899 (63) but were cancelled at the request of the Queen in 1900 in recognition of the loss of life in the Boer War. Following the death of its greatest patron in 1901 the Games were again cancelled.

In 1906 the Duke of Fife gifted to the Society twelve acres of ground in Auchendryne, Braemar, to make a permanent home for the Gathering. It was named The Princess Royal Park and has been in use ever since and has, of course, enjoyed consistent Royal patronage over the years. The present Queen is a regular attender only cancelling in 1979 following the murder of Lord Mountbatten. Instead of the Royal arrival at three in the afternoon there was a one minute silence and a piper played *The Flowers of the Forest.* According to one observer, "All you could hear during the silence was a bairn whimpering".

Participation in the Games is now open to all qualified to take part, not just to locals, and athletes come from all over the world to toss the caber, put the shot and throw the hammer. One activity, the race up Craig Clunie, was ceased at the request of Queen Victoria. It seems that Malcolm Canmore's competition to find the fleetest of foot messenger was a little too exacting: the Queen's ghillie won the race but, along with other competitiors, spat blood such was the exertion required.

This century Balmoral has been used through six reigns with little real change. Edward VII spent a limited amount of time at Balmoral, around three or four weeks a year. Whether this was because he was much taken up with his foreign travels and enjoyment of the fleshpots (40) or just possibly Balmoral, for him, was still haunted by the ghost of the hated John Brown. In any case, his happiest days had been spent at Abergeldie Castle (41) where there had been sparkling house parties with shooting by day and cards by night, and where he had entertained his legendary lover Lillie Langtry. His preferred country home was Sandringham which was nearer to London and the sort of life he was more inclined to lead. In younger days he had been a keen deer-stalker and shot — on one day in 1866 he killed no less than seven stags in a single day's stalking on Craig-na-gall and in the corrie of Baultchach (36). Dissolute living, however, was to catch up with him and by the end of the century he was no longer up to the ardours of a day's stalking. By now he was content to forsake the sport on his Scottish estate for the less demanding shooting of driven pheasants at Windsor and Sandringham.

By Edwardian times, the ladies were not quite so subserviently accepting their roles as "shotgun widows". Lillie Langtry attended a house party at nearby Glentanar Lodge as a guest of Sir William Cunliffe-Brooks. She observed that the men were all "eager for the massacre of grouse and the stalking of deer. They, no doubt, hugely enjoyed themselves killing things, but there is nothing much for women to do, unless they also shoulder a weapon". The resourceful Lillie, however, devised a game for the ladies to play one boring afternoon — tobogganning on tea trays down the stairs — which was entered into with gusto until Sir William, upon his return home from beastly pursuits, ordered the butler to lock up all the silver trays.

In many ways the Edwardian period was one marked by the letting off of steam in the wake of the end of the long Victorian era. George V and Queen Mary brought with them a quite different attitude and way of doing things and, although interrupted by the war years of 1914—18, Balmoral came back into favour as a family retreat. The inks with Scotland were also reinforced with the engagment of the Duke of York to Elizabeth Bowes-Lyon and trips north were prefaced with or punctuated by visits to her home in Angus. George V had been a keen fisherman — "I love a gun but I am never so happy as when I am fishing the pools of the Dee with a long day ahead of me". But the Royal family were, for the first time, beginning to realise that Blamoral was not quite the Highland hideaway it once had been. The motor car had made Deeside more accessible and large numbers of spectators now turned up when the King and Queen went to church of a Sunday, turning it into what one of his biographers called "a peep show".

These trends did not worry the Royal couple over much for there was much change in the wind. The first Labour Party ministers came to Balmoral and the tradition was established of the weekend visit of the Prime Minister. The King was relaxed in the environment of Balmoral and reinforced the traditions established by his grandmother.

The death of King George V in 1936 brought about the tragic and short reign of Edward VIII as uncrowned King. He spent only two disastrous weeks at Balmoral in September and was obliged to issue an official denial to rumours that the Castle would be relegated to the role of shooting lodge. The Court Circular of September 24 1936 recorded that a Mrs Simpson and her friends, Mr and Mrs Herman Rogers, had gone to Balmoral as guests of the King. The nature of Mrs Simpson's relationship with the King was as yet generally unknown and, in his own words, "Now that I had the property, I wanted the others to see it and enjoy with me its famous sport and amenities. Naturally, Wallis was included in the party . . . the days were spent 'on the hill' or the moors: in the evening one relaxed with bridge or the latest films". In the King's view the stay was "extremely pleasant" and "entirely normal".

In fact, the visit was a disaster. Other members of the Royal family, staying elsewhere on the estate, felt deeply insulted by the arrangements generally and, specifically, at Wallis Simpson acting as hostess at Balmoral. The King's brothers felt themselves neglected by the house party at Balmoral — "shut out of his confidence" was the phrase used. The Duke of York, it is said considered himself "to have lost a friend *(in his father)* and to be rapidly losing another in his brother".

There was also a tactless side effect in Edward VIII's travelling into Aberdeen to meet Wallis Simpson from the train. The day she reached Aberdeen Station was the day of the opening of the new Aberdeen Royal Infirmary. The Duke of York performed the ceremony as the King met his lady friend from the train. In fact, earlier in the year the King had taken the view that because of court mourning for his father he could not perform the ceremony and had asked his brother to deputise. But this was not known by Aberdonians who assumed that His Majesty had neglected the opening of the hospital so that he would be free to meet his guest.

The abdication of the King in the following December, following the divorce of Wallis Simpson in October, brought the Duke of York an unanticipated accession to the throne as George VI. As Queen Mary drily observed,

"It is my younger son who is making the sacrifice". As Balmoral was the personal property of the monarch and passed by will to each succeeding King or Queen, George VI was (rather tediously) obliged to actually buy Balmoral from the Duke of Windsor. According to Lord Beaverbrook, the sum involved for Balmoral and Sandringham exceeded one million pounds — which was undoubtedly an unlooked for outlay for the new King. Balmoral effectively supplied the Duke and Duchess of Windsor with their 'pension'.

Fortunately, King George VI regarded Balmoral and its traditions as something to be retained and treasured at all costs. The 1937 Braemar Cathering, the first of the new reign, attracted a record attendance of 25,000 people showing no diminution in the attraction of royalty on Deeside. He threw himself into the organisation of the Estate with real enthusiasm and in 1939 the last of the Duke of York's camps, which brought together boys from widely differing backgrounds, was held on Deeside. As if to usher in a new era of informality, there was tea for the boys at Balmoral and the King personally led them on expeditions into the hills.

During the Second War the Royal family was able to visit Balmoral on a number of occasions and in 1941 the Canadian Premier, Mackenzie King, had talks there with the King. After the war he took a personal interest in all the varied aspects of the running of the estate including improvements, leases and even the employment of staff. He took pleasure in the grouse shooting and stalking and it has often been suggested that the relaxed atmosphere of Deeside served to lengthen his life. But the strain of illness eventually told and in September of 1951 doctors were summoned to Balmoral and advised the King to repair to London as quickly as possible. He was never to return to the Highland estate he had learned to love so much.

Princess Elizabeth had grown up with Balmoral. She was obviously taking an active interest in the place as can be seen from some early pictures of her at the 1927 Balmoral fête (64). She was a regular visitor, along with her sister Margaret Rose, during the 1930s and 40s and it is said that marriage was proposed to her at Balmoral in 1946. One thing is certain and that is that Her Majesty Queen Elizabeth and HRH the Duke of Edinburgh probably take as much interest in their Highland estate as did Victoria and Albert almost one and a half centuries ago.

The Estate is run very much as any similar business today with very few concessions towards the status of the proprietors. During the months of May, June and July the grounds, and an exhibition in the ballroom, (152) are open to the public who, upon payment of a commercial but fair admission fee, can tread the same turf as the Royals will surely do during August and September. There are two well stocked souvenir shops (144) selling a wide range of goods, many of them bearing the image and the name of Balmoral. Tea towels, mats, plates, shortbread, lucky white

An aerial view of Balmoral taken from the helicopter delivering the Royal mail (1949).

heather, books and postcards jostle for attention and are carried off by visitors eager for a souvenir of their visit to the Highland home of the Royals. Yet everything for sale in these two shops bears the Royal seal of approval and, in so far as is possible, is unique to Balmoral: when the shops first opened there was a certain backwash of resentment from traders in nearby Ballater about the commerical activities up at the Castle and Her Majesty has always been properly sensitive to local feeling. Monies taken also form the basis of donations to local charities. Once inside what is, for most of the year, "forbidden territory" under the nearest thing to a security blackout, the visitor is, quite surprisingly, allowed to wander at will around the grounds with virtually no let or hindrance. The windows of the Castle itself, however, defy the gaze of the most persistent of prying eyes: the windows at ground floor level are all firmly closed off by shutters or blinds and the entrance porch is closed up against any entrant by enormous oak doors. In the greenhouses and conservatories there is ample evidence of the preparation of plants and flowers for the forthcoming Royal visit: all, apparently, delicately timed to flower from mid-August onwards! The exhibition in the ballroom gives a glimpse of what life is like behind the shuttered windows of the main building: there are Victorian photographs and paintings of the interior of the Castle but, essentially, it remains an exclusive, private place. And, at the beginning of August, the exhibits in the ballroom will be cleared away and restored to their normal place within the Castle: the ballroom will be available, once again, for the annual Ghillies' Ball.

The Balls are given every year for estate workers, locals and soldiers making up the Royal Guard (they allegedly spend weeks being instructed in the non too gentle art of the Scottish reel in anticipation of a Royal request for the pleasure of a dance). The dancing at the Ghillies'Ball is energetic: those to whom Scottish country dancing is an undiscovered pleasure might view it as being positively rough. But Her Majesty loves every minute and is especially fond of the Eightsome Reel and the Duke of Perth. All the members of the Royal party participate in the reels and enjoy the essential democracy of Scottish country dancing: it is one of the few dance forms which actually ensures you will meet virtually everybody else in the room, irregardless of their circle of friends or station in life. Currently, the Jack Sinclair Band start to play just after 10 p. m. and Her Majesty dances for around two hours with estate workers and soldiers in the intimate atmosphere of the small ballroom.

The Royal *penchant* for Scottish country dancing led to a general resurgence of interest post-war. Not only were they danced enthusiastically at the Ghillies' Ball but members of the Royal family, especially Princess Margaret Rose, patronised the balls which formed an integral part of the Deeside season. Her favourite dance at the Aboyne Ball, which she attended on many occasions, was Hamilton House and one observer recorded that "her grace and rhythm were a joy to watch". The Aboyne Ball in the early 1950s was the finale to a week of Games and balls with, right up to the mid-50s, the Aberdeen *Press & Journal* listing house parties from more than two dozen country houses in Aberdeenshire: minor European royalty, English and Scottish aristocracy, London debs and assorted socialites flocked to the wilds of Deeside to be beside the Royals and the social events which took place in their orbit. As the Aberdeen paper reported the Aboyne Ball of September 1951, "The lights gleamed on diamonds and pearls, on rich, shimmering gowns, silver buttons, *skean dhus* and all the traditional finery of a Scottish ball" (104).

But, even after a Ball, everyone at Balmoral is up sharp to greet the new day. One regular guest at Balmoral describes it as "bloody hard work" and a stay there certainly would not accord with many people's ideas of a restful holiday. Gentlemen are expected to be out shooting or fishing by 0830 hours, ladies can either go out riding with the Queen around 10.00 or, alternatively, follow the shoot. Guests under no circumstances are allowed to dally inside, whether or not they secretly wish to slide down the stairs on silver tea trays!

The Queen is particularly fond of organising picnics and some evenings there are barbecues. After dinner (prompt at 8.30 p. m.) there is often some compulsory group activity like *Charades*, which is particularly popular, or *Trivial Pursuits*. Sometimes there is a sing-song around the piano and house guests are well advised to practise their party pieces before a stay at Balmoral!

For Prince Philip many days are spent on the Estate (138) in which he takes a personal interest. In 1955 he introduced Highland Cattle and, in 1966, a herd of Luing Cattle, Shorthorns crossed with Highland (142). In 1972 this stock was supplemented with a herd of Galloways. The Balmoral estate is, in relative terms, a small estate and the rendering of it economic is a considerable challenge. This is a challenge to which the present Royal family have willingly risen.

The Prince of Wales has inherited his parents'love of Balmoral. At one time he used to shoot grouse three or four times a week each autumn, he is also a keen fisherman and one summer day in 1976 he landed seven salmon when the river was generally thought to be too low to merit the effort. A number of years ago he wrote a children's story based on the surrounding area for the amusement of his younger brothers. *The Old Man of Lochnagar* was later published in aid of charity and was a considerable success.

Balmoral also provided the backdrop to whet was arguably the love affair of the 1980s — the marriage of the Prince of Wales to Lady Diana Spencer. In 1979 Lady Diana was a guest of Prince Andrew at Balmoral: that same summer when the terrible news of the assassination of Earl Mountbatten by Irish terrorists broke. By the following year she was the secret girlfriend of the Prince of Wales, was again in the Balmoral house party and, one month later, she was staying at Birkhall with the Queen Mother. There can be little doubt about the central role played by Balmoral in the Royal romance.

Part of the Royal honeymoon was spent on Deeside (154) and, subsequently, the couple have made their holiday home at Craigowan Lodge on the estate, just ten minutes walk away from the Castle. Here they can enjoy a greater degree of privacy than anywhere else and although the Princess of Wales is an energetic girl easily given to boredom, they are happier there than the popular press gives them credit.

As the twentieth century grinds remorselessly to a close there is every indication that the Castle and estate of Balmoral remain as firmly fixed in the affections of the British Royal family as they have ever been. As the Prince of Wales once remarked of Queen Victoria, "She hated leaving, much as I hate leaving this marvellous place".

A HOME IN THE HIGHLANDS

Bringing the Stags Home. Oil by Carl Haag, 1854. By gracious permission of Her Majesty the Queen.

The Royal Party fording the Tarff, Glen Tilt. Watercolour by William Leitch, 1861. By gracious permission of Her Majesty the Queen.

An enthusiastic Scottish dance on board the Royal yacht *Victoria and Albert* en route to Scotland in August 1847. Queen Victoria and Prince Albert had already begun their love affair with Scotland.

Queen Victoria and Prince Albert pictured at the time they took over the Balmoral Estate.

The Royal arrival at the port of Aberdeen for the first visit to Balmoral in 1848. The Royal party has just passed through the first of a series of triumphal arches. The Royal yacht arrived so far ahead of schedule that the arch was hurriedly completed only minutes ahead of the Queen stepping ashore, and the Lord Provost and other members of the reception party (pictured here) had to be summoned by special messengers.

4 The old Balmoral Castle, which was built between 1834 and 1839 by Sir Robert Gordon, was initially leased by the Royal family from the trustees of the Duke of Fife. It quickly proved too small for Royal requirements. This photograph was taken by George Washington Wilson in September 1854, shortly before its demolition.

5 The new Balmoral Castle, Prince Albert's grand Scottish *schloss*, under construction. The building was designed by the Prince Consort in association with William Smith of Aberdeen. This photograph was taken from the north by Washington Wilson in September 1855.

6 The drawing room at Balmoral Castle, 1857, from a watercolour by J Roberts. "Tartanitis" is much in evidence in the carpets, curtains and soft furnishings. In the servants' quarters the linoleum, even, bore a tartan design.

7 Queen Victoria's sitting room at Balmoral from a photograph by Washington Wilson (1875).

8 Queen Victoria's dressing room at Balmoral (Washington Wilson, 1875). Again, note the tartan carpet and tablecloth.

9 The bedroom of Queen Victoria and Prince Albert at Balmoral. There is a photograph of Prince Albert to the right of the bed: this picture of him on his deathbed was to the right of any bed in which Queen Victoria slept (Washington Wilson, 1875).

10 The dining room, as pictured by *The Graphic* in 1882, with the Queen at the head of the table.

11 The ground floor corridor at Balmoral, pictured by *The Graphic* in 1882. The Royal guard is to the left and on the right is the statue of the Prince Consort by William Theed.

12 *Overleaf:* Balmoral Castle from across the fast-flowing River Dee (Washington Wilson).

13 On September 29 1855 Aberdeen photographer George Washington Wilson was summoned to Balmoral to take this historic Royal engagement picture. Prince Frederick of Prussia had proposed to Vicky, the Princess Royal, then aged only 14. *Left to right:* Prince Alfred, Prince Frederick William of Prussia, Princess Alice, The Prince of Wales, Queen Victoria, Prince Albert, and Victoria, Princess Royal.

BALMORAL CASTLE, FROM

RIVER. 99. G.W.W.

14 A picnic in the Highlands, October 16 1861. Artist Carl Haag accompanied the party and pictured, left to right, Princess Alice, her fiancé Prince Louis of Hesse, Princess Helena, the Prince Consort and Queen Victoria. This was to be the last happy Scottish expedition before the Prince Consort died.

15

The massive statue of the Prince Consort which was unveiled on October 11 1867. It is an enlarged copy of the statue by Theed within the Castle corridor and shows Prince Albert in Highland costume, with plaid and kilt and with a double-barrelled shotgun in his right hand and his left resting on his favourite gundog.

16

Following the death of Prince Albert, a funeral hatchment was erected on the castle above the *porte cochère.* The diamond-shaped board bore the full heraldic achievement of the Prince and was one of a series of hatchments which the widowed Queen commanded to be displayed on all Royal residences. In Scotland, the other building to bear a hatchment was the Royal Palace of Holyroodhouse in Edinburgh. The hatchments remained on display during the period of official mourning: this photograph was taken in 1861.

17 The grieving widow is pictured before a painting of the Prince Consort in the drawing room at Balmoral. To her left is Princess Helena and to her right Princess Louis of Hesse (formerly Princess Alice). The photograph was taken in October, 1863.

18 Taken at the same time as the photograph overleaf, this one shows the Queen with her granddaughter, Princess Victoria Mary of Hesse, the eldest child of Princess Louis of Hesse, and grandmother of the present Duke of Edinburgh.

19 Members of the Royal family gathered at Balmoral in September 1887. *Left to right:* Prince Albert Victor of Wales, Princess Alix of Hesse (later the Czarina), Queen Victoria, Princess Henry of Battenburg (formerly Princess Beatrice), Princess Irene of Hesse, and Bosco, Prince Henry of Battenberg's dog.

20 Queen Victoria took delight in the daily drives at Balmoral. Here she is pictured with Princess Louise and Princess Beatrice. On the box are John Brown and the coachman Bourner.

21 The Royal party on the steps at Balmoral, May 25 1868. Left to right: Prince Leopold, Queen Victoria, Princess Beatrice, Prince Arthur, Princess Louise and the Prince of Wales, Above, on the steps, is the Duchess of Atholl.

22 Inside the tent erected for the Ghillies' Ball given by Queen Victoria for Princess Christian's birthday on May 25 1868. On the dais are, left to right: the Duchess of Atholl, Princess Beatrice, Queen Victoria, Princess Louise, the Prince of Wales, Prince Leopold and Prince Arthur.

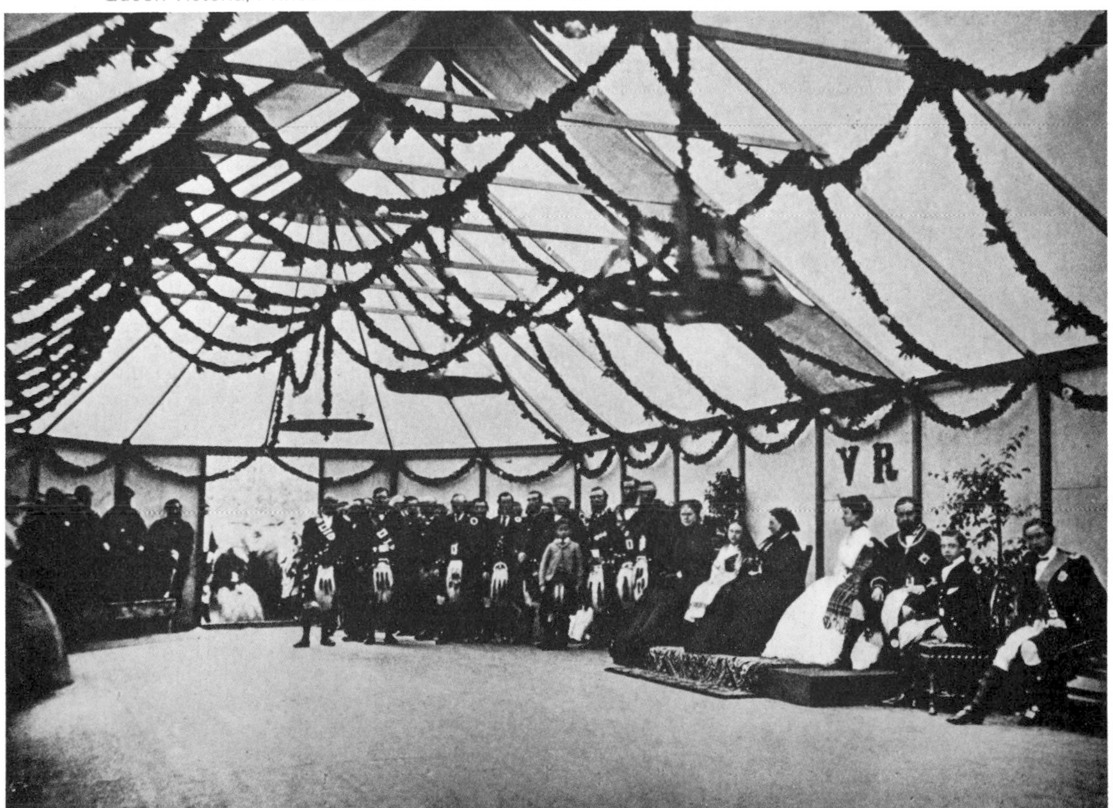

23

At Balmoral in September 1878 are, left to right: Princess Louise, Prince Leopold, Queen Victoria, the Marquis of Lorne and Princess Beatrice.

24

An October 1876 photograph of Queen Victoria wit[h] Prince Arthur, Duke of Connaught, Princess Beatric[e] and Spot the dog.

25 This photograph, popularly reproduced in Victorian times, is usually known as "The Four Princes". Taken at Abergeldie on September 1 1881, during the residence of the Prince of Wales at Abergeldie Castle, it portrays H.R.H. The Prince of Wales, H.R.H. the Duke of Edinburgh, H.R.H. the Duke of Connaught and H.R.H. the Duke of Albany.

26 *Left:* Again dominated by the impassive figure of the Queen, this October 1882 photograph shows family and dogs at Balmoral. Left to right: the Grand Duke of Hesse (Prince Louis), Princess Beatrice, little Princess Alix of Hesse, the Hereditary Grand Duke of Hesse, the Duchess of Connaught and her daughter, Princess Margaret. Staying remarkably still in front are the dogs Wat, Gay Girl and Spot.

27 Queen Victoria's Balmoral letter paper bore this engraving of roebuck, designed by Sir Edwin Landseer in the mid-1850s.

28 Balmoral letter paper with an engraving of deer, also designed by Sir Edwin Landseer.

29

A September 1897 photograph of Queen Victoria preparing to go out for her afternoon drive. *Left to right:* George Gordon, the pony Bella, the Duchess of Roxburghe, the Queen (with her dog Turi) and one of her Indian servants, Mohammed Ismail.

30

Gelder Shiel

31

The summer house by Loch Muick much favoured by Queen Victoria, Glassalt Shiel.

32 Another 1897 photograph of Queen Victoria with, left to right: Princess Victoria Eugenie of Battenberg, Princess Francis Joseph of Battenberg and the Duchess of York.

33 Queen Victoria's birthday presents laid out at Balmoral, 1898.

34

The Queen with the Prince of Wales, Princess Victoria of Wales and Prince Edward of York.

35 The three Victorias at Balmoral: the Queen with granddaughters Princess Victoria of Wales (left), daughter of the Prince of Wales, and Princess Victoria of Schleswig Holstein, the first daughter of Princess Helena, Duchess of Saxony.

36 The Prince of Wales shooting grouse at Balmoral, August 1881.

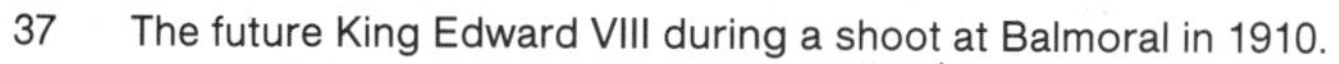

37 The future King Edward VIII during a shoot at Balmoral in 1910.

38 Birkhall was purchased by Prince Albert in 1849 as an additional, adjacent residence for his eldest son. The home for successive Princes of Wales, it is now the Deeside home of the Queen Mother.

39 King Edward VII pictured at Balmoral in 1901 with his grandchildren. Prince Albert (the future King George VI), on the right, is just six years old.

40 The leisure activities of King Edward whilst Prince of Wales had incurred the displeasure of his mother. His travels, gambling and succession of lady friends brought much comment both overt and covert. This irreverent cartoon was published in 1905 picturing him, complete with Highland dress, with "friends" in Paris.

41 *Overleaf:* Abergeldie Castle which was leased to the Royal family from 1848.

N-FRONT, ABERGELDIE

E. 656 G.W.W.

42 While Edward VII was staying at Balmoral, Abergeldie Castle was occupied by the Prince of Wales and family. This picture was taken there in the autumn of 1905. The young Prince John is seen in his mother's arms.

43 This picture was taken at Balmoral in 1911 and shows Prince Albert, the future King George VI, standing on Princess Mary's right. Also in the picture is Prince George (extreme left), Prince Henry and Prince Edward.

44 At Balmoral for the Braemar Gathering, September 1921. The Duke of York is to the right, the Prince of Wales on the left and, in the middle, the Earl of Athlone. On the extreme left is the boy Duke of Norfolk, Earl Marshall of England, who was to play such an important role in the constitutional crisis of 1936 and the ultimate coronation of the Duke of York as George VI.

45 With Queen Mary at Balmoral in 1923, Prince George and the newly married Duchess of York (Elizabeth Bowes-Lyon) and Duke of York.

46 Queen Mary arrives at Ballater Station, August 1925.

47 King George V inspects the traditional Guard of Honour upon arrival at Ballater Station.

8 The young Princesses, Margaret and Elizabeth, arrive at Ballater Station, 1932.

9 It was announced from Balmoral on August 28 1934 that the youngest son of the King and Queen, the Duke of Kent, had become engaged to Princess Marina of Greece. The engagement took place in Bled, in northern Yugoslavia at the summer home of the Yugoslav Royal Family, Vila Bled. The couple then travelled to England and thence to Balmoral where this official engagement picture was taken on September 18. Pictured before the *porte cochère* are the two Royal families, left to right: Princess Nicolas of Greece, King George V, Princess Marina, Prince George, Queen Mary and Prince Nicolas of Greece. Princess Marina was Prince Nicolas's youngest daughter (born 1906).

50 King Edward VIII, tragic uncrowned King.

INSTRUMENT OF ABDICATION

I, Edward the Eighth, of Great Britain, Ireland, and the British Dominions beyond the Seas, King, Emperor of India, do hereby declare My irrevocable determination to renounce the Throne for Myself and for My descendants, and My desire that effect should be given to this Instrument of Abdication immediately.

In token whereof I have hereunto se My hand this tenth day of December, nineteen hundred and thirty six, in the presence of the witnesses whose signatures are subscribed

SIGNED AT
FORT BELVEDERE
IN THE PRESENCE
OF

Edward R.I.

Albert

Henry.

George.

52 The instrument of abdication, December 1936.

51 King Edward VIII inspects the Guard of the 1st Battalion the Gordon Highlanders, under the command of a Major D. Hunter. Blair at Ballater Station, September 20 1936.

53

Queen George V and Queen Mary go to Crathie Church, 1935.

54

August 1939 and an era draws to a close as the Royal family goes to church at Crathie in a horse-drawn carriage for the last time. Facing King George VI and Queen Elizabeth are the two young Princesses, Elizabeth and Margaret. The era of the horseless carriage — and the onset of war — are now virtually upon the Royal family.

55 King George VI looks through the eyepiece of a Movietone News cine camera at Abergeldie, August 4 1939.

56 An early convert to the cine camera, here King George VI films at Balmoral in August 1939 as the two young Princesses look on.

GUESTS & HOSTS

Hallowe'en Party at Balmoral. Watercolour by W E Green, 1882. By gracious permission of Her Majesty the Queen.

The Ghillies' Ball at Balmoral. Watercolour, 1859. By gracious permission of Her Majesty the Queen.

The sons of The Prince of Wales: Prince Henry, Prince Albert and Prince George, Balmoral, 1910.

The Duke and Duchess of York with Queen Mary, Balmoral, 1924.

57 During the 19th century the links between the Royal families of Europe were very close. This photograph was taken at Balmoral in September 1884 on the occasion of the visit of the Crown Princess of Germany (Queen Victoria's eldest daughter). *Left to right:* the Duchess of Edinburgh with her daughters the Princess Marie (later to become Queen of Rumania), Victoria Melita and Alexandra, Queen Victoria, Princess Victoria of Prussia and her mother the Crown Princess of Germany.

58 Another photograph which serves to emphasise the German links of the Royal family at the time. This 1895 picture shows, left to right, back row: Princess Helena Victoria of Schleswig Holstein, Prince Henry of Battenberg, Count Mensdorff, Princess Henry of Battenberg and the Duke of York. Seated next to Queen Victoria are the Duchess of York and Prince Edward. *Front row, left to right:* Princess Victoria Eugenie of Battenberg, Prince Waldemar of Prussia, Prince Alexander of Battenberg.

59 Visiting circuses were popular with the Royal family during the 1890s and they were regularly encamped in the grounds of Balmoral during the summer. This group of contortionists, a clown and a bareback rider were all members of Sanger's Circus which performed there in June 1898.

60 "Lord" George Sanger was particularly proud of his white elephant, "the only white elephant ever seen in the Western world". But when pressed by the Prince of Wales on the matter he ruefully admitted that it was only white because it was whitewashed every day!

Fijian warriors on a visit to Balmoral in 1904 were as much of an object of curiousity as Sanger's white elephant.

10/9/04.

On September 10 1927 some 3,400 people attended a fête held in the grounds at Balmoral. There were seven large marquees full of stalls and in this picture crowds are making for the marquees. King George V sold flowers for almost three hours — with considerable commercial success. The object of the fête was to liquidate an £800 debt outstanding on Crathie Hall.

WELCOME

63 The annual Highland Gathering was held at Balmoral in 1899 and this photograph shows the elaborately decorated Royal pavilion and the Royal party within.

64 The Princess Elizabeth is wheeled in a pram at the Balmoral fête of 1927. She was described by the *Press & Journal* correspondent as "a winsome child with big wandering blue eyes and golden curls". Behind are the King and Queen followed by the Duke and Duchess of York and Lord and Lady Carnegie.

65 Queen Mary pictured at the Balmoral fête.

66 A photograph to celebrate the visit of the American President, President Eisenhower, to Balmoral, August 28 1959. *Left to right:* the Duke of Edinburgh, the Princess Anne, President Eisenhower, Her Majesty the Queen, Prince Charles, Major John Eisenhower. Secret servicemen ('G Men' in the parlance of the *Press & Journal*) accompanying the President clearly found Balmoral something of a security challenge: "In huge blue and silver USAF Chevrolet cars they roared along the twisting roads that surround Balmoral. Six or seven men to a car, crew-cropped, grim unsmiling, all in loose white raincoats, they stopped every now and then to search moors and riverbank".

67 Queen Elizabeth and Princess Margaret chat to members of the Australian team at Balmoral.

68 The Australian cricket team was invited to spend the weekend at Balmoral in 1948. Here is Don Bradman, the Australian captain, in extraordinarily casual pose with the King. His hands-in-pocket stance attracted much unfavourable comment at the time.

69 King George VI has a go at the Aunt Sally at the King's Camp, Abergeldie, August 1939. As Duke of York he had inaugurated these annual camps in 1919, bringing boys from industry and public schools together as his guests. The August 1939 camp was attended by 200 boys and each day the King led the boys on an expedition. The boys were invited to tea at Balmoral and a new era of Royal informality was ushered in.

ROYAL DEESIDE

The Duchess of York with the young Princesses and Duchess of Gloucester, Crathie Sale of Work, 1936.

Princess Elizabeth and the Prince of Wales, Crathie Church, 1933.

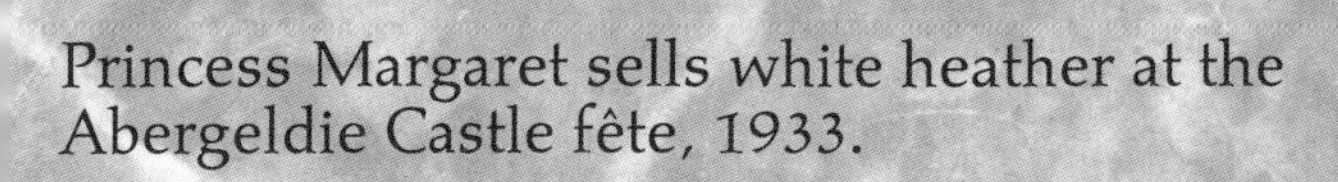

Princess Margaret sells white heather at the Abergeldie Castle fête, 1933.

A View of Balmoral. By James Giles, 1848. By gracious permission of Her Majesty the Queen.

Crathie Church from across the River Dee.

70 Pictured by the artist from *The Graphic* in 1882, the old Crathie Church (1804) across the river from Balmoral Castle was attended regularly by Queen Victoria ever since her first Sunday on Deeside.

71 The interior of the old church at Crathie, showing the Queen's pew in the centre of the gallery. It was demolished to make way for the present building in 1893.

72 The Crathie Bazaar of 1894 was organised by the Royal family in order to raise money for the building of a more adequate Church. Many of the stalls were manned by members of the Royal family and all the Royals staying at Balmoral donated crafts and other goods. More than £1200 was raised.

73 Queen Victoria lays the foundation stone of the new Crathie Church, September 11 1893.

74 King George VI and Queen Elizabeth, together with the young Princesses, go to Crathie church for service, August 1937.

75 King George V leaves Crathie Church, 1932.

76 Outside Crathie Church in the rain, 1934, and a closed carriage is *de rigeur*!

77 Queen Elizabeth and the Princesses patronise the Crathie Sale of Work, September 1945.

78

Her Majesty the Queen at the Crathie Sale of Work, 1953.

79 The Balmoral Gathering of 1898.

80 The Gathering was held in the grounds of Braemar Castle in 1895 and in this picture John Lamond prepares to toss the caber. The Royal tent is in the middle distance.

81 Four Kings and a Queen at the Braemar Gathering of 1902. *Left to right:* Queen Alexandra, Duke of York (later King George V), Colonel Farquharson, King Edward VII, Prince Albert of York (George VI) and Prince Edward (Edward VIII).

82 In the Royal Pavilion at the 1937 Gathering. *Left to right:* the Marquis of Aberdeen, King George VI, Queen Elizabeth, Princess Elizabeth, Princess Margaret and Prince and Princess Arthur of Connaught.

83 Going to the Braemar Gathering of 1937 in an open carriage drawn by greys.

84 The Royal party arrives at the 1933 Braemar Gathering.

85 The archway under construction at Princess Royal Park, Braemar, for the 1937 Games.

86 The magnificent setting of the Braemar Gathering is clearly illustrated by this 1959 picture of the crowd and events arena.

87 During the Braemar Gathering of September 1950 the King and Queen broke with tradition and left the Royal Pavilion to walk in the arena to watch the events and chat with the competitors. This was the first time this had happened since the days of Edward VII and it delighted the 30,000 strong crowd. *Left to right:* Queen Elizabeth, King George VI, the Marquess of Aberdeen, Lord Carnegie and the young Prince Michael of Kent.

88 The 1946 Games at Braemar.

89 The two young Princesses at the 1938 Games.

90 Two older Princesses at the 1946 Games.

91 Raincoats and umbrellas at the 1950 Games.

92 A discussion over *cromachs* at the 1948 Games.

94 The Royal party at the 1962 Games.

95 The Royal party at the 1961 Games.

93 March past of the massed Pipe Bands, 1961. A stirring and traditional feature of the Gathering.

96

The King and Queen enjoy a joke at the 1951 Gathering.

97 The 1955 Braemar Gathering marked the debut of Prince Charles and Princess Anne at the event. The crowd were delighted when they appeared dressed in the Balmoral tartan, designed by Prince Albert and also worn by the Duke of Edinburgh.

98 A word in granny's ear from Prince Charles at the 1957 Gathering.

99 Princess Elizabeth and Princess Margaret arrive at Ballater Station, August 1948.

100

August 1949 and it is Prince Charles' first visit to Scotland. The young Prince arrives at Ballater Station to be met by the Marquess of Aberdeen.

101

Prince Charles and Princess Anne arc among the Royal party arriving at Ballater Station, August 3 1951.

102

Princess Margaret passes her driving test at Ballater, 1949.

103 Princess Elizabeth and Princess Margaret visit the circus at Ballater, August 1945, continuing a long tradition of Royal patronage of circuses on Deeside.

104

Princess Margaret dancing one of the square dances at the Aboyne Ball of September 1951. The *Press & Journal* described it as "a brilliant finale to Games Week on Deeside" with some 280 people dancing the night away in the Victory Hall at Aboyne. Princess Margaret wore a gown of billowing white tulle with a Stuart tartan sash secured by two diamond brooches. "Her grace and rhythm were a joy to watch". She was partnered by her cousin, the Master of Elphinstone.

105 August 31 1951 and King George VI inspects the Guard at Ballater Station on his last visit to Balmoral. He is a sick man. Before the end of his visit doctors will be summoned to Balmoral and he will have to go back to London, never to return.

106 On August 20 1955 the Queen Mother organised a fete at Abergeldie Castle to provide a new vestry for Crathie Kirk, continuing a long tradition of Royal support and assistance. Her Majesty the Queen and Prince Philip, wearing the Balmoral tartan, are pictured at the fete which raised £2,200.

ROYAL RETAINERS

The Ballroom, Balmoral Castle.

The south front, Balmoral Castle.

Statue of Queen Victoria erected by estate workers to mark her Jubilee.

The Tower, Balmoral Castle.

107 Highland ghillies on the Balmoral Estate, 1856.

108 Ghillies and foresters pose with a stag shot by Prince Albert, October 5 1854.

109 Queen Victoria and John Brown, Balmoral, 1863.

TO

MY LOYAL HIGHLANDERS

AND ESPECIALLY

TO THE MEMORY OF

MY DEVOTED PERSONAL ATTENDANT

AND FAITHFUL FRIEND

JOHN BROWN

THESE RECORDS OF MY WIDOWED LIFE

IN SCOTLAND

ARE

GRATEFULLY DEDICATED

VICTORIA R. I.

111

The dedication to *More Leaves from the Journal of a Life in the Highlands* which unequivocally indicated the Queen's affection for her servant.

110 As the Queen's personal attendant, John Brown became her almost constant companion. Here he is pictured, by Sir Edwin Landseer (1886), with Queen Victoria at Osborne House on the Isle of Wight.

112 John Brown's Death Certificate.

CERTIFIED COPY OF AN ENTRY OF DEATH

(6 & 7 Wm. IV., cap. 86).

[illegible]

REGISTRATION DISTRICT

1883. DEATH in the Sub-District of

No.	When and Where Died. (1)	Name and Surname. (2)	Sex. (3)	Age. (4)	Rank
154	Twenty seventh March 1883 Windsor Castle	John Brown	Male	56 years	Person Attend Her Ma Que

CERTIFIED to be a true Copy of an Entry in the Certified Copy of a

Given at the General Register Office, Somerset House, London,

[illegible]

D 02131

3 Queen Victoria and John Brown outside the stables at Balmoral.

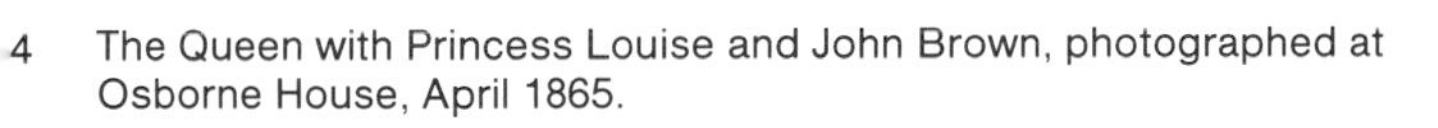

4 The Queen with Princess Louise and John Brown, photographed at Osborne House, April 1865.

115 The Queen commissioned this painting from Charles Burton Barber (1876) and presented it to John Brown.

GIVEN AT THE GENERAL REGISTER OFFICE,
SOMERSET HOUSE, LONDON.

Application Number 22664

r in the Counties of Berks and Surrey

Cause of Death. (6)	Signature, Description and Residence of Informant. (7)	When Registered. (8)	Signature of Registrar. (9)
Erysipelas, 4 days Certified by James Reid M.D.	Archd. Brown Brother Present at the Death 19 Victoria Street New Windsor	Twenty eighth March 1883	Geo. W. Plumridge Registrar

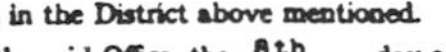

s in the District above mentioned.

the said Office, the 8th day of April 19 37.

Will. IV., c. 86, sec 38; 34 & 25 Vict., c 98, sec. 38; 1 & 2 Geo V., c 6, sec 4; 3 & 4 Geo V., c 27, sec. 3, 5 & 6
rting to be Sealed or Stamped with the Seal of the General Register Office, shall be received as evidence of the Birth
y; and no Certified Copy purporting to be given in the said Office shall be of any force or effect which is not Sealed

d certificate as true, knowing it to be false, is liable to Prosecution.

116 Queen Victoria with her Hindu secretary Munshi Hafiz at Balmoral in the 1890s.

117 Queen Victoria presents the Colours to the Cameron Highlanders at Balmoral, October 29 1898. The Empress Frederick of Germany and Prince Henry of Battenberg are in the carriage with the Queen.

118 The Tsar of Russia visited Balmoral in September 1896 and this fascinating photograph was taken of the senior members of the two Royal households. *Back row, left to right:* Mlle Wassilitchikoff, Col. the Hon. William Carington, Count Worontzoff-Daschkoff, Sir Arthur Bigge, Dr James Reid, General Sir Stanley Clarke, Sir Arthur Davidson. *Middle row:* Jane, Lady Churchill, Edith, Lady Lytton, M. de Staal, the Hon Harriet Phipps, Count Benckendorff. *Front row:* Lord Pembroke, Prince Galitzin, Baron Churchill, Lord Edward Clinton and M. Dubreuil Eschapper.

119 Prince Albert, destined to become George VI, walks in the drive at Balmoral with his tutor, Mr Hansell, 1911. Edward VII died that year and his father became King. Mr. Hansell also taught Prince Edward to shoot (*q. v.* 37). Prince Albert wears a black mourning band on his left arm.

120 An official photograph of members of the Aberdeen County Constabulary on Royal Guard duty at the Braemar Gathering in 1921. The two plainclothes gentlemen are assumed to be 'undercover' men who mingled with the crowd.

121 A tongue in cheek photograph of members of the Royal household attending King George V and Queen Mary at Balmoral in 1920. *Left to right:* Telephonist, Confectioner, Court Telegraphist, Chef, Court Postmaster and a Footman.

122 The Guard of Honour is largely a ceremonial institution. The King or Queen were always greeted by a detachment at Ballater Station upon arrival for the Balmoral stay. Here battledress is worn in the aftermath of war (August 8 1946).

123 Loading the Royal mail into a helicopter at Dyce Airport for the early morning run to Balmoral, August 1947. It is, of course, essential that papers and dispatch boxes reach Her Majesty promptly.

124 The colours of the 4th/7th and 5th/6th Battalions The Gordon Highlanders are marched off for the last time, August 18 1961.

125 August 18 1961 and Her Majesty the Queen presents new colours to the 3rd (T. A.) Battalion The Gordon Highlanders at Balmoral Castle. As Her Majesty said, "This ceremony is, so to speak, on home ground for everyone". Her Majesty is accompanied by Lt. Col J Shankley, officer commanding.

126 Nurse Helen Lightbody holds Prince Charles by the hand and Princess Anne, in shawl, Aberdeen Joint Station, October 1950.

127 October 1951 and Princess Anne has clearly grown. Nurse Lightbody looks after the children, a job she carried out with remarkable efficiency over a long period of devoted service. Initially, she was employed as nanny to the sons of the Duke and Duchess of Gloucester and later went to work for the Queen. As nanny to the Royal children she herself had an assistant, a nursery maid, two nursery footmen and a chauffeur. She came to the job through answering an advertisement in a nursing magazine.

MODERN TIMES

The approach to the Castle by the main drive

The west front of the castle.

The north front with tower and ballroom to the left.

128 Prince Charles and Princess Anne at Ballater Station, 1954.

129 “Come along then!” Prince Charles at Ballater Sation, 1950.

130 Princess Anne and Prince Andrew at Ballater, 1962.

131 Her Majesty the Queen inspects the Guard of Honour at Ballater Station, 1962.

132 Princess Anne travels up front in a battery railcar on the Royal Deeside line between Aberdeen and Ballater, 1959.

133 Princess Anne's first visit to Scotland, September 1950. Pictured at Ballater Station are the Princess (with Nurse Lightbody), Princess Elizabeth, Prince Charles and Provost Adams.

134 The time spent by the Royal family at Balmoral means that there are many official suppliers of goods and services on Deeside. One of the most unusual must be Robin Fraser Callander, drystane dyker to H M The Queen. He is charged with the maintenance and repair of the many old stone walls on the Balmoral Estates.

135 William Moir of Aberdeen spends about a fortnight every year at Balmoral servicing and repairing the 70 clocks. Official clock repairer to the Queen is just one of his appointments — he also looks after all the town clocks in Aberdeen and here he is in the Town House, Aberdeen, Hogmanay, 1972.

136

H M Sheridan of Ballater is well known as the local butcher but also holds three Royal warrants as purveyor of meat and poultry to H. M. The Queen, H. M. the Queen Mother and H.R.H. The Prince of Wales. The butchery business was started in the premises in 1868 and there have only been four owners of the Bridge Street shop in that time. Pictured *(above right)* is the shop around 1900.

137

The staff of H M Sheridan are pictured outside the shop in this recent photograph. *Left to right:* Vince Duguid, Michael Sheridan (Proprietor), Ronnie Gray, William Johnstone *(Partner)*, Barry Florence, John Sinclair and Michael Law.

J & D Murray of Ballater are chemists to H M The Queen and H M The Queen Mother. The shop's most popular line is *Ironside's Emollient Skin Cream*, made by the Murrays in Ballater.

138 Her Majesty the Queen and HRH The Duke of Edinburgh take a deep interest in the administration of the Balmoral Estates and, within a few days of their arrival, a tour of the various activities is arranged. Here they are seen speaking with the Estate's ranger-naturalist (1977).

139 Her Majesty's delight to be back on Deeside is plain from this 1978 photograph of her inspection of the Guard of Honour of the Black Watch at the gates of Balmoral Castle.

140 Her Majesty at the meeting of the British Drawing Society at Balmoral (1977).

141 This attractive and informal 1979 study of the Royal family in the grounds at Balmoral was taken by *Press & Journal* photographer Bob Bruce. *Left to right:* Prince Edward, Her Majesty The Queen, Prince Andrew, The Prince of Wales and the Duke of Edinburgh.

142 Farm grieve Robbie Anderson looks after the Balmoral herd, the Castle in the background.

143 At the stables, to the side of the Castle, Martin, one of the Fell ponies used by the Duke of Edinburgh in three-day eventing, appears to enjoy his daily wash-down (1982).

144 For three months of the year the policies of Balmoral are opened to the public and are a popular tourist draw. This is the interior of one of the bright, attractively laid out souvenir shops which sell a wide range of Balmoral-branded goods.

145 Visitors to Balmoral are transported around the estate on a cart pulled by a pair of ponies. It is actually a converted Edinburgh milk float!

146 Painters get to work in preparation for the arrival of the Royal party (1984).

147 The logistics of moving the Royal family and its household up to Scotland are formidable. Here a Freightliner unloads around 20 tons of personal luggage.

8
sitors admire the ponies at the Royal stables: the area around
lmoral is first class for pony trekking.

149 The sunken garden to the west of the Castle, with the shuttered rooms of the Queen's suite beyond.

150 The circular game and venison larder, adorned with a frieze of antlers. Slits in the wall provide ventilation. The stables and estate offices are on the extreme left.

151 In 1987 new staff quarters, a canteen, recreation rooms and a cafeteria for the public were opened. The attractive new complex, located between the main house and the stables, replaced a corrugated iron building put up during the reign of Queen Victoria.

152 In 1980/81 the ballroom at the Castle was prepared to house an exhibition of paintings, porcelain, photographs and some furniture illustrative of the history of the Royal Highland home. Pictured shortly after the opening is the display area with Miss Brenda Collie, the Queen's housekeeper, and Keeper Sandy Booth. The ballroom is actually quite small but provides a homely and comfortable setting for the annual Ghillies' Ball.

153 Pictured in May 1981, the Prince of Wales and his fiancée, Lady Diana Spencer, on a quiet holiday at Balmoral.

154 The honeymoon picture of the Prince and Princess of Wales on the banks of the River Dee at Invercauld (August 1981). The transformation to Royal Princess in just a few months is quite startling when the two photographs are compared.

155 The Castle has its own Dennis fire engine and crew of volunteer firefighters, including estate workers and Miss Brenda Collie.

ROYAL ABERDEEN

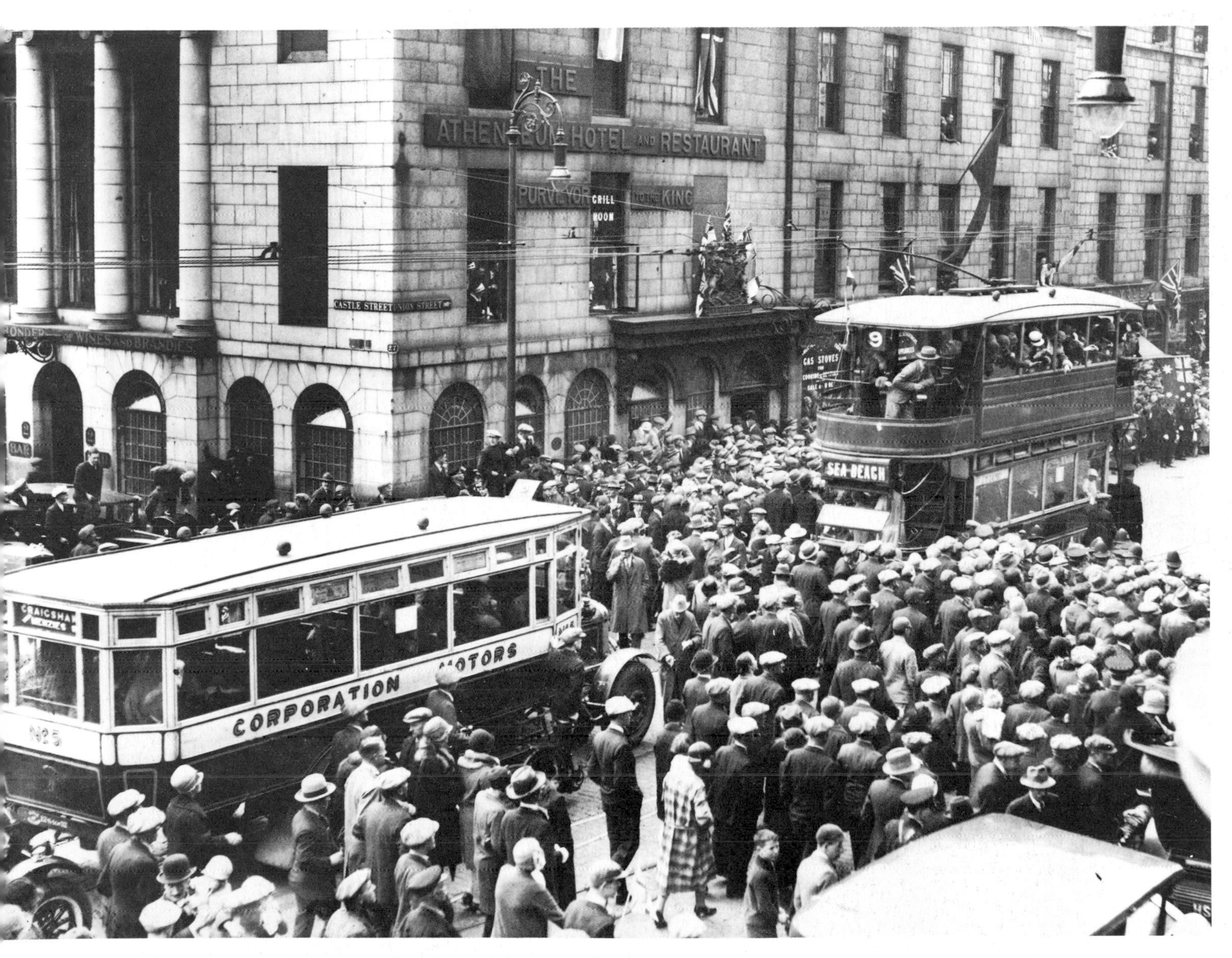

156 Ever since Balmoral became Queen Victoria's Highland home, Aberdeen has enjoyed particularly close links with successive monarchs, who are almost constantly passing through the City to and from Royal Deeside. Here crowds are gathering in Union Street for the visit of the Prince of Wales in 1928.

157 The Prince of Wales' car crosses the Brig of Balgownie in 1928.

158 Lord Provost Thomas Mitchell is flanked by the King and Queen at the opening of the new King George V Bridge over the River Dee at Aberdeen (March 10 1941).

159

September 24 1936 and the opening of the Royal Infirmary, Aberdeen, by the Duke and Duchess of York.
The absence of King Edward VIII caused comment at the time.

August 1938 Royal arrival in Aberdeen by sea. The Royal party is met by the Lord Provost and councillors.

161 The Royal barge berths at Aberdeen, August 4 1938, and King George VI, Queen Elizabeth, Princess Margaret and Princess Elizabeth step ashore.

162 Princess Margaret's first public engagement was at Dyce on September 16 1945 where she inspected local youth organisations.

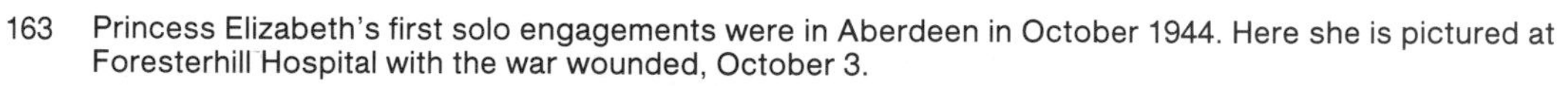

163 Princess Elizabeth's first solo engagements were in Aberdeen in October 1944. Here she is pictured at Foresterhill Hospital with the war wounded, October 3.

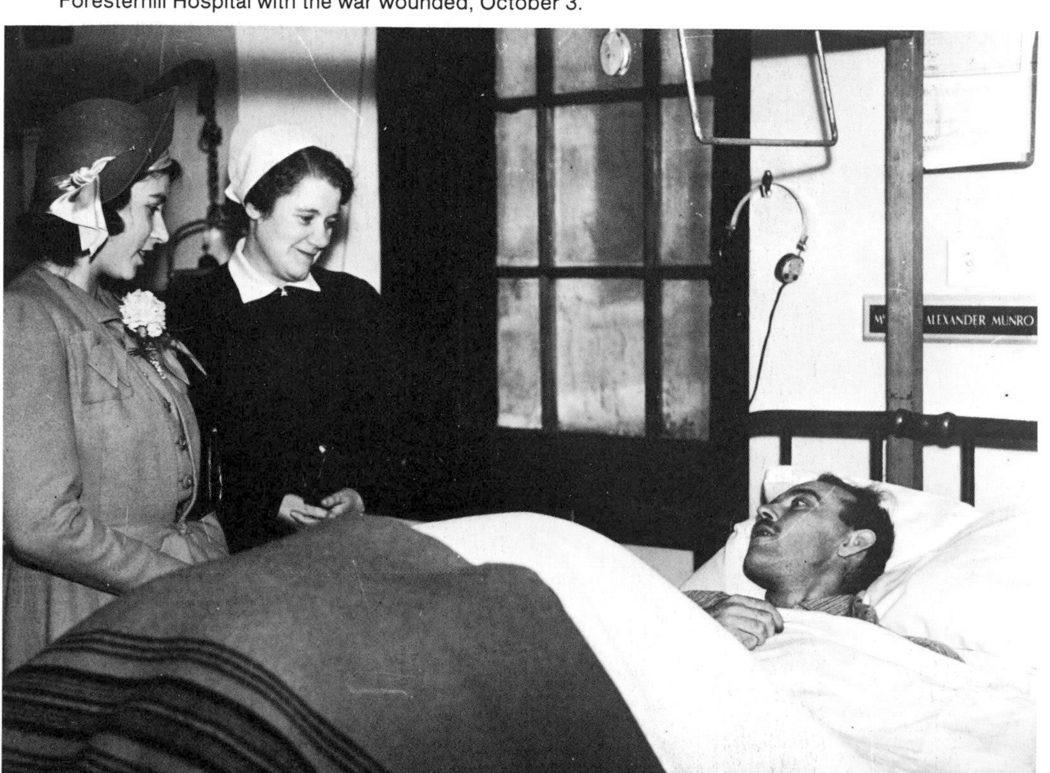

164 Lord Provost Thomas Mitchell welcomes Princess Elizabeth to the Sailors' Home in Aberdeen where she opened an extension in October 1944.

165 The comings and goings of the Royal family by train have been a favourite subject for press photographers over the years. In this charming October 1956 picture Prince Charles and Princess Anne are at the window of the Royal train, in their pyjamas, before leaving Aberdeen for London.

166 Teddy gets a look out of the window at Aberdeen Joint Station (October 1951).

167 Prince Charles has a cuddle for Princess Anne, Aberdeen Station, October 1951.

168 *Right:*
Princess Elizabeth and Princess Margaret leave the Aberdeen Joint Station for London, October 1950.

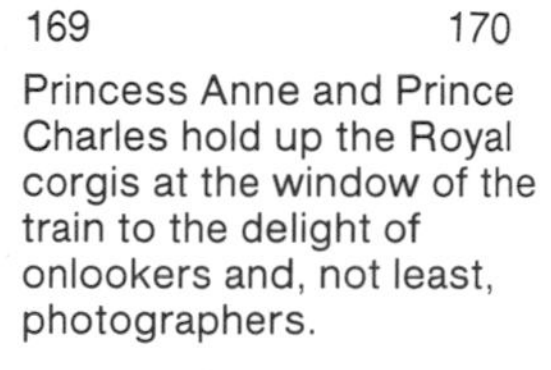

169 170

Princess Anne and Prince Charles hold up the Royal corgis at the window of the train to the delight of onlookers and, not least, photographers.

171 Photographed in 1938 the Royal yacht *Victo & Albert III* which brought the Royal fam to Aberdeen on so ma occasions. The third Royal yacht bearing th name *Victoria and Albert*, she was completed in 1899 bu was never used by Queen Victoria as she took a strong dislike t the vessel after protracted constructi problems. She becam the official Royal yach of King Edward VII an was the largest and most magnificent roya yacht in Europe at the time. She served King George V and VI and was withdrawn from service shortly before the outbreak of the Second World War.

172 Leaving the Royal yac *Britannia*, berthed at Aberdeen, in 1955. Th was *Britannia's* first tr to Aberdeen, following a successful cruise around the Western Isles. She was completed on the Clyc by John Browns in 19 and her 15.5 foot draught allows her to up at the quayside in Aberdeen.

173

The Queen Mother opens Provost Skene's House after extensive refurbishing in September 1953.

174

The Duke and Duchess of Kent arrive at Dyce Airport after their wedding in June 1961.

175

Her Majesty the Queen was literally besieged at Aberdeen Town House when she made her famous "all clear" visit in 1964 after the typhoid outbreak in the city. Her visit was deeply appreciated by the citizens of Aberdeen who displayed their affection in dramatic fashion.

176 Her Majesty departs from Aberdeen's Dyce Airport, May 1978, with the Royal corgis. Looking on is Bill Aitkenhead, airport manager.

177 The Queen Mother attended the 150th Anniversary of the Royal Horticultural Society of Aberdeen in September of 1974. Pictured with her, in Duthie Park, are Lord Provost John Smith, the Lady Provost (behind) and Mrs E Finlayson, chairman of the Royal Horticultural Society of Aberdeen.

178 The Queen Mother with Prince Andrew and Prince Edward on the Deeside Road, August 1973.

Evening Express
LATE FINAL
Day to remember as Queen Mother drops in to see news in the making
A ROYAL HELLO
Inside your 'EE' tonight
Pretty as a picture in blue
Pictures by CHARLES FLETT and ROBERT BRUCE
ROSSLEIGH FOR QUALITY
NEW & USED CARS
NEW CARS
USED CARS
ROSSLEIGH
THE QUALITY CAR SPECIALISTS
383 UNION ST ABERDEEN
Jack WILSON
THE MAN FOR CARS
NEW VOLKSWAGENS

SUGGESTED FURTHER READING

There exists, of course, a plethora of reading matter dealing with the subject of the Royal Family. These suggestions for further reading are selected for their relevance to the subject of this book and/or because they are, in my view, particularly interesting.

Books

Brown, Ivor: ***Balmoral***, Collins, London & Glasgow, 1955
Clark, Ronald W: ***Balmoral: Queen Victoria's Highland Home***, Thames & Hudson, London & New York, 1981
Crabtree, Reginald: ***Royal Yachts of Europe***, David & Charles, Newton Abbot & Vancouver, 1975
Duff, David: ***Victoria in the Highlands***, Frederick Muller, London, 1968
Farr, A Derek: ***Stories of Royal Deeside's Railway***, Kestrel, Knaresborough, 1971
Lindsay, Patricia: ***Recollections of a Royal Parish***, London, 1902
McConnochie, Alex Inkson: ***Queen Victoria's Highland Home and Vicinity***, Aberdeen, 1897
Martine, Roddy: ***Royal Scotland***, Paul Harris Publishing, Edinburgh, 1983
Martine, Roddy: ***A Royal Tradition: The Queen and her Family in Scotland***, Mainstream, Edinburgh, 1986
Russell, Peter, and James, Paul: ***At Her Majesty's Service***, Collins, London, 1986
Stirton, Rev. John: ***Balmoral in Former Times: an Historical Sketch***, Forfar, 1921
Tisdall, E E P: ***Queen Victoria's John Brown***, Stanley Paul, London, 1938
Tschumi, Gabriel: ***Royal Chef***, William Kimber, London, 1954
Victoria, H.M. Queen (ed. Helps, Sir Arthur): ***Leaves from the Journal of Our Life in the Highlands from 1848—1861***, John Murray, London, 1868
Victoria, H.M. Queen (ed. Murray MacGregor): ***More Leaves from the Journal of a Life in the Highlands from 1862—1882***, London, 1884
Windsor, HRH the Duke of: ***A King's Story***, London, 1951
Whittle, Tyler: ***Victoria and Albert at Home***, University of Queensland Press, St Lucia, 1980
Wyness, Fenton: ***Royal Deeside***, Alex. P Reid & Son, Aberdeen, 1968

Newspapers & Periodicals

The files of the ***Press & Journal*** and ***Evening Express*** (Aberdeen), ***Scottish Annual, and Book of the Braemar Gathering***

179 *Opposite:*
The Queen Mother holds aloft a rapidly produced copy of the *Evening Express* given to her at the end of her visit to Aberdeen Journal's new premises in Lang Stracht in 1974.

SOURCES OF PICTURES

Front cover photograph by Paul Harris
Back cover photographs (colour) by Paul Harris; half tone, Aberdeen Journals Ltd.
1 Author's Collection
2 Aberdeen Journals Ltd
3 Author's Collection
4 Author's Collection/George Washington Wilson
5 Author's Collection/George Washington Wilson
6 Author's Collection/after J. Roberts
7 Author's Collection/Washington Wilson
8 Author's Collection/Washington Wilson
9 Author's Collection/Washington Wilson
10 Mary Evans Picture Library/*The Graphic*
11 Mary Evans Picture Library/*The Graphic*
12 Author's Collection/Washington Wilson
13 Author's Collection/Washington Wilson
14 Aberdeen Journals Ltd/after Carl Haag
15 Aberdeen Journals Ltd
16 Charles Burnett Esq/Washington Wilson
17 Author's Collection/Washington Wilson
18 Author's Collection
19 Author's Collection/Watson
20 Author's Collection/Whitlock
21 Author's Collection/W & D. Downey
22 Author's Collection/W & D. Downey
23 Author's Collection/Washington Wilson
24 Author's Collection/Washington Wilson
25 Mary Evans Picture Library/Robert Milne, Ballater
26 Author's Collection/Washington Wilson
27 Author's Collection/Sir Edwin Landseer
28 Author's Collection/Sir Edwin Landseer
29 Author's Collection/Milne
30 *More Leaves from the Journal of a Life in the Highlands*
31 *More Leaves from the Journal of a Life in the Highlands*
32 Author's Collection/Milne
33 Aberdeen Journals Ltd/Milne
34 Author's Collection/Milne
35 Aberdeen Journals Ltd/Milne
36 Mary Evans Picture Library/*Illustrated London News*
37 Author's Collection
38 Aberdeen Journals Ltd
39 Author's Collection
40 Mary Evans Picture Library/Bruno Paul in *Simplicissimus*, 1905
41 Author's Collection/Washington Wilson
42 Author's Collection
43 Author's Collection
44 Author's Collection
45 Author's Collection
46 Aberdeen Journals Ltd
47 Aberdeen Journals Ltd
48 Aberdeen Journals Ltd
49 Aberdeen Journals Ltd
50 Author's Collection/after a photograph by Hugh Cecil
51 Aberdeen Journals Ltd
52 Aberdeen Journals Ltd
53 Aberdeen Journals Ltd
54 Aberdeen Journals Ltd
55 Aberdeen Journals Ltd
56 Aberdeen Journals Ltd
57 Author's Collection/Watson
58 Author's Collection/Milne
59 Private Collection/Milne
60 Private Collection/Milne
61 Archive Publications Ltd
62 Aberdeen Journals Ltd
63 Private Collection/Milne
64 Aberdeen Journals Ltd
65 Aberdeen Journals Ltd
66 Aberdeen Journals Ltd
67 Aberdeen Journals Ltd
68 Aberdeen Journals Ltd
69 Aberdeen Journals Ltd
70 Mary Evans Picture Library/*The Graphic*
71 Mary Evans Picture Library/*The Graphic*, from a photograph by J. Crowder
72 Aberdeen Journals Ltd/Milne
73 Aberdeen Journals Ltd/Milne
74 Aberdeen Journals Ltd
75 Aberdeen Journals Ltd
76 Aberdeen Journals Ltd
77 Aberdeen Journals Ltd
78 Aberdeen Journals Ltd
79 Aberdeen Journals Ltd/after Milne
80 Aberdeen Journals Ltd/after Milne
81 Aberdeen Journals Ltd
82 Aberdeen Journals Ltd
83 Aberdeen Journals Ltd
84 Aberdeen Journals Ltd
85 Aberdeen Journals Ltd
86 Aberdeen Journals Ltd
87 Aberdeen Journals Ltd
88 Aberdeen Journals Ltd
89 Aberdeen Journals Ltd
90 Aberdeen Journals Ltd
91 Aberdeen Journals Ltd
92 Aberdeen Journals Ltd
93 Aberdeen Journals Ltd
94 Aberdeen Journals Ltd
95 Aberdeen Journals Ltd
96 Aberdeen Journals Ltd
97 Aberdeen Journals Ltd
98 Aberdeen Journals Ltd
99 Aberdeen Journals Ltd
100 Aberdeen Journals Ltd
101 Aberdeen Journals Ltd
102 Aberdeen Journals Ltd
103 Aberdeen Journals Ltd
104 Aberdeen Journals Ltd
105 Aberdeen Journals Ltd
106 Aberdeen Journals Ltd
107 Author's Collection/Fenton
108 Aberdeen Journals Ltd/Washington Wilson
109 Author's Collection
110 Aberdeen Journals Ltd/*Reproduced by Gracious Permission of Her Majesty the Queen*
111 *More Leaves from the Journal of Our Life in the Highlands*
112 Somerset House, London
113 Aberdeen Journals Ltd/George Washington Wilson
114 Author's Collection
115 Aberdeen Journals Ltd/Sotheby's/Charles Burton Barber
116 Mary Evans Picture Library/*Illustration London News* after Milne
117 Aberdeen Journals Ltd/Milne
118 Private Collection/Milne
119 Author's Collection
120 Aberdeen Journals Ltd
121 *Royal Chef* by Gabriel Tschumi
122 Aberdeen Journals Ltd
123 Aberdeen Journals Ltd
124 Aberdeen Journals Ltd
125 Aberdeen Journals Ltd
126 Aberdeen Journals Ltd
127 Aberdeen Journals Ltd
128 Aberdeen Journals Ltd
129 Aberdeen Journals Ltd
130 Aberdeen Journals Ltd
131 Aberdeen Journals Ltd
132 Aberdeen Journals Ltd
133 Aberdeen Journals Ltd
134 Aberdeen Journals Ltd
135 Aberdeen Journals Ltd
136 Messrs H M Sheridan of Ballater
137 Messrs H M Sheridan of Ballater
138 Aberdeen Journals Ltd
139 Aberdeen Journals Ltd
140 Aberdeen Journals Ltd
141 Aberdeen Journals Ltd/Bob Bruce
142 Aberdeen Journals Ltd
143 Aberdeen Journals Ltd
144 Aberdeen Journals Ltd
145 Aberdeen Journals Ltd
146 Aberdeen Journals Ltd
147 Aberdeen Journals Ltd
148 Aberdeen Journals Ltd
149 Aberdeen Journals Ltd
150 Aberdeen Journals Ltd
151 Aberdeen Journals Ltd
152 Aberdeen Journals Ltd
153 Aberdeen Journals Ltd
154 Aberdeen Journals Ltd
155 Aberdeen Journals Ltd
156 Aberdeen Journals Ltd
157 Aberdeen Journals Ltd
158 Aberdeen Journals Ltd
159 Aberdeen Journals Ltd
160 Aberdeen Journals Ltd
161 Aberdeen Journals Ltd
162 Aberdeen Journals Ltd
163 Aberdeen Journals Ltd
164 Aberdeen Journals Ltd
165 Aberdeen Journals Ltd
166 Aberdeen Journals Ltd
167 Aberdeen Journals Ltd
168 Aberdeen Journals Ltd
169 Aberdeen Journals Ltd
170 Aberdeen Journals Ltd
171 Newcastle Chronicle & Journal
172 Aberdeen Journals Ltd
173 Aberdeen Journals Ltd
174 Aberdeen Journals Ltd
175 Aberdeen Journals Ltd
176 Aberdeen Journals Ltd
177 Aberdeen Journals Ltd
178 Aberdeen Journals Ltd
179 Aberdeen Journals Ltd

COLOUR PLATES

Plate I Author's Collection
Plate II Paul Harris
Plate III Reproduced by Gracious Permission of Her Majesty the Queen (Windsor Castle Royal Library)
© Copyright H. M. The Queen
Plate IV Reproduced by Gracious Permission of Her Majesty the Queen (Windsor Castle Royal Library) © Copyright H. M. The Queen
Plate V Reproduced by Gracious Permission of Her Majesty the Queen (Windsor Castle Royal Library) © Copyright H. M. The Queen
Plate VI Reproduced by Gracious Permission of Her Majesty the Queen (Windsor Castle Royal Library) © Copyright H. M. The Queen
Plate VII Author's Collection
Plate VIII Author's Collection
Plate IX Reproduced by Gracious Permission of Her Majesty the Queen (Registrar of the Royal Collection) © Copyright H. M. The Queen
Plate X Paul Harris
Plate XI Paul Harris
Plate XII Paul Harris
Plate XIII Paul Harris
Plate XIV Paul Harris

Photographic vignettes on title page and in introduction by Paul Harris. Other photographs in introduction by Aberdeen Journals Ltd